# THE ELK

BY
## MARK E. AHLSTROM

EDITED BY
## DR. HOWARD SCHROEDER

**Professor in Reading and Language Arts
Dept. of Elementary Education
Mankato State University**

---

PRODUCED AND DESIGNED BY
## BAKER STREET PRODUCTIONS
**Mankato, MN**

# CRESTWOOD HOUSE

Mankato, Minnesota

# CIP

## LIBRARY OF CONGRESS CATALOGING IN PUBLICATION DATA

Ahlstrom, Mark E.
  The elk.

  (Wildlife, habits & habitat)
  SUMMARY: Discusses the life cycle of the elk, its characteristics, habitat, environment, predators, and its place in our world today in relation to man.
  1. Elk--Juvenile literature. (1. Elk) I. Schroeder, Howard. II. Baker Street Productions. III. Title. IV. Series.
QL737.U55A35     1985          599.73'57          85-11667
ISBN 0-89686-278-X (lib. bdg.)

| **International Standard Book Number:** | **Library of Congress Catalog Card Number:** |
|:---:|:---:|
| Library Binding 0-89686-278-X | 85-11667 |

## ILLUSTRATION CREDITS:

Lynn M. Stone: Cover, 8, 13, 20, 23, 34-35
Mark Newman/Tom Stack & Assoc.: 4
George J. Sanker/DRK Photo: 7
Lynn Rogers: 10, 19, 30-31, 37
Nadine Orabona: 14
G.C. Kelley/Tom Stack & Assoc.: 16, 40-41
Tom Bean/DRK Photo: 24-25
John Shaw/Tom Stack & Assoc.: 26
Rod Planck/Tom Stack & Assoc.: 29
Gary R. Zahm/DRK Photo: 32
Phil & Loretta Hermann: 38
Tom Stack/Tom Stack & Assoc.: 43
Jerg Kroener: 45

## CRESTWOOD HOUSE

Hwy. 66 South, Box 3427
Mankato, MN 56002-3427

# TABLE OF CONTENTS

"Holy smokes, *what* was *that*?" you whisper to your friend after you regain control of yourself.

"That, my friend, is what you came for," he replied.

The day had begun very early. When you poked your head out of your dew-covered tent, the stars were still twinkling in the sky. You shivered as you pulled on

*A bull elk at dawn.*

4

your jeans, and then headed out of the tent to get a campfire started.

After a few cups of coffee had cleared away some of the cobwebs in your mind, you started to get excited. Very excited! You were in the Bob Marshall Wilderness Area in western Montana, and were about to see something that you had been dreaming about for years. To be here on this frosty fall morning, you had travelled a thousand miles. You were going to see elk during the bugling season! While it was still dark, you had walked up to a large mountain meadow. You were watching an elk herd in the half-light of dawn.

Planning for the trip began months before, back home in Minnesota. Your friend had called and suggested the trip. He said he would take care of getting horses and all of the camping gear. All you had to do was bring a warm sleeping bag and personal items. It was an offer that you just could not refuse.

But to be sure that you would understand what you would be seeing, you had decided to do some reading. In fact, you had done a lot of reading! The more you read, the more excited you got. You also jogged, and rode horses on weekends to get in shape.

When at long last the day to leave arrived, you felt that you were ready. You had paid special attention to your clothing. Because you would be "packing-in" on horses, you had to be selective. And yet you had to be ready for all kinds of weather. Fall in the mountains could bring anything from blizzards to 70° "bluebird" days. By being careful, all of your clothing had fit into a large duffel bag.

After kissing the family goodbye, you drove west. You had taken your time, enjoying the changing seasons. The greens of summer were slowly giving way to the golds of fall. You found yourself whistling tune after tune as the miles rolled by—first the farmlands, then the prairies and ''badlands'' of the Dakotas. Finally, you had slowly climbed into the mountains of the American West.

When you had arrived in western Montana two days later, your friend greeted you with a smile and a hug. ''Well, let's get rolling,'' he said. ''The horses are waiting.''

After a short drive to a nearby ranch in your friend's pickup truck, you loaded the horses into a trailer. With the trailer in tow, you headed into the mountains. You drove until the road stopped. Because it was late, and you had a full day's ride ahead, you decided to camp for the night.

You watched in amazement as your friend lashed camping gear and duffel bags onto the pack horse the next morning. What a balancing act! Finally, you set out. Three horses and two people heading for the home of the elk.

As you moved further from the trail head, the mountains grew larger and larger. The trail crossed small streams and rock slides as it wound higher into the mountains. The timber became thicker, but every once in awhile there were large open spaces. The grass in these mountain meadows was still a rich green color. Your friend explained that you would be seeing elk in meadows, such as these, higher up the mountain.

*A bull elk bugles in a mountain meadow.*

Towards sundown, you had reached a nice little meadow near the top of the mountain. A small stream crossed the meadow. "This will be our home for the week," your friend said. As you got off your horse to stretch your aching muscles, you looked back. You felt you were on top of the world! It seemed like you could see for hundreds of miles.

When the time came to crawl into your sleeping bag, you fell asleep immediately. You had not heard your friend say that he would wake you at 4:00 a.m.

So that's what got you to this time and place, when the strange sound of a bugling bull elk startled you.

What a sound that bugle is! It can send chills up and down your spine, no matter how many times you hear it. Norm Strung, an outdoor writer, describes the bugle of the bull elk this way: "The cry of the loon, the honk of a goose, and the howl of a coyote are mere noise by comparison."

Let's take a closer look at this grand animal.

— M.E.A.

*An elk feeds on mountain grasses at sunset.*

# CHAPTER ONE:

# The elk came from Asia

If you had been living in Minnesota a couple of hundred years ago, it would have been easy to see a bugling elk. Elk were everywhere. In fact, before white people came to North America, there were elk from coast-to-coast. The herds also ranged south into Mexico and across much of western Canada.

Biologists believe that Asia is the original home of the elk (which is called *Cervus elaphus* by biologists). Some of the animals moved west into Europe thousands of years ago. Today, these animals are called Eurasian red deer. The animals we know as North American elk spread slowly. They moved through Siberia, and then across a landbridge that is believed to have once connected Siberia to Alaska. From Alaska, they fanned out across much of North America. All of this movement, of course, didn't happen "overnight." It took a very long time. Although there was once some doubt, biologists now believe that all elk living in Europe, Asia, and North America are the same animal. In this book, however, we will focus on the North American elk.

# Sometimes known as "wapiti"

The elk is the second-largest member of the deer family. In North America, that includes moose (the largest deer), elk, caribou, mule deer, and whitetail deer. When the first English settlers came to the eastern

*Like all members of the deer family, only the males have antlers.*

coast of the United States, they saw two types of deer. The smaller ones they called "deer." Today we know them as whitetail deer. They called the larger ones "elk" because they didn't know better!

Most of the settlers had been poor, city people in their homeland. They knew little about wildlife. Some of them had no doubt heard about a large-horned animal known in Europe as an elk. Obviously, they had never seen the European elk. At any rate, that's why they started calling the large North American animal an elk.

After a number of years, settlers who did know something about wildlife started arriving. They soon saw that the "elk" was not properly named. For in Europe, "elk" is the word used to describe the animal we know in North America as the moose. These settlers wanted to avoid the confusion. Because they didn't think it was a red deer (we now know it was the same), they decided a new name would be in order. The experts chose the local Indians' name for the animal—wapiti. Many people, however, continued to call the animals elk.

Neither "wapiti" nor "elk" was ever officially recognized. Today, both terms are used. Elk is used in this book because it is the most common of the two terms.

# The many types of elk

The best estimate is that there were about ten million elk at the time the white man came to North America. As was said earlier, their range extended from coast to coast. Biologists have identified six subspecies, or types, of elk that lived in different parts of North America. They are: Eastern, Manitoban, Merriam, Tule, Rocky Mountain, and Roosevelt. All except the Eastern and Merriam elk still exist in North America today. (Note: it may be helpful to look at the map on page 46.)

The Eastern elk, which is now extinct, once had the largest range of all the types. These elk once lived in what biologists call the eastern deciduous forest. The border of their range ran from New England to the Great Lakes region. It then ran south almost to the Gulf of Mexico and eastward to the Atlantic coast. Because elk cannot live without wilderness, civilization meant the end of this type of elk. They gradually died out as the settlers moved westward. By 1850, most of the Eastern elk were gone.

Manitoban elk lived in a band between the Rocky Mountains and the eastern deciduous forest. This is the area known as the Great Plains. Their range extended north into Saskatchewan and Manitoba, Canada, south as far as Texas. Civilization almost wiped out this type,

*Some Manitoban elk still live on the plains of Canada.*

too. Today, Manitoban elk live only in a few small parts of Manitoba and Saskatchewan.

Merriam elk were once found in the mountain ranges of Arizona, New Mexico, Texas, and Mexico. There were never great numbers of this type in Mexico, and they were probably extinct by the 1700's. In the United States, their decline came more slowly. The end came when the elk could no longer compete with domestic cattle. The limited amount of grass in their range made it impossible. The last of the Merriam elk were seen in the early 1900's. These were the largest of all the elk. The bulls had the biggest antlers.

Tule elk are the ''little guys'' of the elk world. They are the smallest of the subspecies. Their range once extended across much of central California. Until the 1850's, there were large herds of Tule elk living in the semidesert valleys and foothills. As people irrigated the land to grow crops, these elk were forced out. Only good game management allows them to exist in a few scattered areas today.

*Tule elk of California are the smallest subspecies of elk.*

Rocky Mountain elk originally had a range that extended from the northern borders of British Columbia and Alberta, Canada to the southern borders of Nevada and Colorado. As their name suggests, they lived in the Rocky Mountains and nearby mountain ranges. Because they lived in such a rugged area, they were not bothered much when western North America was settled. The same is true today. In fact, where they have good habitat, their numbers are increasing.

Of the types still in existence, Rocky Mountain bulls have the biggest antlers. Because this raises their status as a game animal, Rocky Mountain elk are often selected for transplant programs. We'll talk about these programs later in the book.

Roosevelt elk have the largest body size of all the types. Bulls as large as one thousand pounds (475 kg) have been recorded. Although people have forced them out of some areas, their range is pretty much the same as it has always been. They live in the mountains along the Pacific Coast from northern California to Vancouver Island in Canada. There are also a large number of them now living on Afognak Island in Alaska. This Alaskan herd grew from a small number of Roosevelt elk that were transplanted there in the 1920's.

# The right habitat

As we've seen, North American elk have lived "from sea to shining sea" and almost everywhere else in between. It would seem that about all they can't handle are deserts and swamps.

One other point is painfully clear. Elk refuse to live near people. Humans and elk just don't mix well. That's why the only elk herds that are holding their own are those that live in the mountains.

For elk, the mountains are the final frontier. Our modern way of life has forced the North American elk to make their last stand. They have no where else to go.

*The mountains are the elk's last chance for survival.*

# CHAPTER TWO:

# Member of the deer family

Except for the moose, the elk is the largest antlered mammal in North America. The males, called bulls, will usually weigh between six hundred and eight hundred pounds (273 - 364 kg) when mature. The females, known as cows, weigh between four hundred and six hundred pounds (182 - 273 kg). The young elk are called calves.

Some real "monster" elk have been recorded. Several Roosevelt bulls killed on Afognak Island in Alaska have weighed as much as fifteen hundred pounds (682 kg).

A mature bull will be about five feet (1.5 m) tall and eight feet (2.5 m) long. It will have antlers that are four to five feet (1.2 - 1.5 m) long. Each antler will have six or more "points," or branches. The distance between the antlers can be as much as five feet (1.5 m). The cows have no antlers. (Note: There's more about antlers in the next section.)

Elk have four toes on each foot. The two middle toes are the ones that form the hooves. The two outside toes are "vestigial" toes that have become dewclaws. The dewclaws are high on the elk's foot and do not normally touch the ground. However, when the hooves sink deeply into soft ground, the dewclaws help to support the weight of the elk. The hooves of a mature elk will make prints in the ground that are about three to four inches (7.7 - 10.3 cm) wide.

Elk are covered with hair that is various shades of brown. The hair on the head and neck is chestnut brown. The hair on the tail and rump is a light tan color. The hair on the belly and legs is very dark brown, sometimes almost black. In the fall, elk grow a dense undercoat to help keep them warm during the winter. In the spring, elk molt, or change, their winter coat for a summer coat. During the molt, they look downright awful! The winter coat hangs in loose, shaggy patches. The summer coat that grows in is reddish in color. There is no undercoat. Compared to how they look in their winter coats, the elk are quite sleek looking during the summer months. The elk will start growing their winter coats again in the fall.

Most members of the deer family have thirty-two teeth. Elk have thirty-four. The two extra teeth are "tusks," of sorts, in the upper jaw. They do not seem to have any useful purpose. What is known is that thousands of elk have been killed through the years, just so people could collect the tusks.

How long do elk live? There is no easy answer. There are so many things that cannot be predicted, like disease,

*When elk "molt" their hair in the spring, they are very shaggy looking.*

severe winter weather, and food supply. Only nature can predict these things. Biologists do know that the average elk has the potential to live for about fifteen years. They also know that elk in the wild will not usually live as long as elk in a zoo. A number of wild elk are known to have reached twenty years of age. The all-time record is a twenty-five-year-old bull killed by a hunter in the 1930's in Arizona. Biologists count ''growth rings'' in an elk's teeth to figure their age. It's very much like counting growth rings on a tree stump.

# A special look at antlers

There is really only one reason that bull elk grow those amazing antlers. It's to keep order in the herd. Assuming that he's healthy, the bull with the largest antlers will be "king of the hill." This large bull is usually called the herd bull. No other bulls will seriously fight with him. He just has to show up, wave his antlers around, and the other bulls will usually back off. During the mating season, he will have his choice of cows for

*The bull with the largest horns will usually rule the herd during the mating season.*

mating. The bulls with smaller antlers will not do much mating.

Things can get interesting if a bull with antlers of nearly equal size shows up in the area during the mating season. He will probably want to challenge the herd bull. If they decide to fight, it can look pretty frightening. There will be a lot of noise when they smash their antlers together. Chunks of sod will fly as they paw the ground.

A fight is good though for the elk herd. If the herd bull is losing his edge, the younger and stronger bull will win the fight and the right to do most of the breeding. Chances are good that his offspring will also grow up to be strong animals. We'll take a closer look at these fights in Chapter Three.

Bulls do not start growing antlers until their second year. The first set of antlers will usually be single "spikes." In a healthy herd, the spikes will be about fifteen inches (38.5 cm) long. If conditions are right, these yearlings will sometimes grow two or three points on each antler. But this is rare.

The bull will shed his antlers after the mating season each winter. He will start growing a new set in the spring. If the bull stays healthy, his antlers will get longer and thicker each year. More and more points will also be added onto each of the main beams of the antlers. Growth is most dramatic during the first five or six years. Maximum size is usually reached in twelve or thirteen years. If a bull stays healthy, he will keep his large antlers for another five or six years. From then on, the antlers will usually get smaller each year until the bull dies.

Most mature bulls will have antlers that end in a fork. The Roosevelt elk is an exception. One branch of the fork on a Roosevelt sometimes branches further into a "crown" of three or four more points. An elk with this rare kind of antlers is known as a "royal." An elk with royal antlers is especially prized by people that hunt elk.

Antler growth begins in the spring as the days start to get longer. Biologists believe that the increasing amount of daylight cause the new antlers to start growing. It takes a mature bull between four and five months to grow a full set of antlers. During this time the antlers are covered with a soft growth called "velvet." Blood vessels inside the antlers carry minerals for growth. When antlers first reach their full size they are made of cartilage. Because the antlers are soft and easily damaged during this time of growth, bulls usually go off by themselves.

The cartilage is slowly replaced by bone material. When the antlers have completely hardened into bone, the velvet is shed. It seems that the shedding causes itching. Bulls speed the process by rubbing their antlers on branches and small trees. The velvet is usually shed within a few hours during the early fall. The bulls are then ready to show off their headgear during the coming mating season.

*Two bulls with their antlers in "velvet."*

# Diseases and enemies

Although elk are bothered by a number of diseases, most of them are not fatal. One exception is necrotic stomatitus. This disease hits an elk herd when it is crowded on a winter range. The overcrowding causes a shortage of the right foods. This forces the elk to eat rough forage. The sharp edges of the forage, like stems and seeds, cause puncture wounds in the elk's mouth and throat. The wounds can lead to infections in many parts of the body, sometimes causing death.

*Elk are in the most danger from disease when they are crowded on winter ranges.*

Elk that begin the winter in good condition will usually survive the disease. If, on the other hand, an elk herd was not well fed, most of the herd might die. Biologists have learned to use this disease for the elk's benefit. Experience has told them that when the disease occurs in a seemingly healthy herd, it spells future trouble. It almost always means that there are too many elk in the herd.

Game managers can then try to have hunters harvest a part of the herd. If the size of the herd can be reduced in time, the herd can be saved. If not, most of the herd might die during the winter.

Starvation is the elk's main enemy. People are usually

*Starvation during the winter is the elk's greatest enemy. This antler and skull were found on a winter range in the spring.*

the cause of this problem. Our life-styles have pushed elk into smaller and smaller areas. These areas have only so much food. When there are too many elk in an area, disaster is just around the corner.

Some of the worst situations are in areas that were originally set up to protect wildlife. Yellowstone National Park is such an example. Because of man's decisions to eliminate natural predators like timber wolves and mountain lions, few predators are left to control the size of an elk herd. Laws prevent hunting in the Park by the one ''predator'' that is left—man. Since protected areas, like Yellowstone, often have the biggest herds, it's only a matter of time before nature runs its course.

Sooner or later, a large part of the herd will die during a bad winter in the Park. TV crews will come running, and for a short time a lot of people will get concerned. The matter is soon forgotten, however, because everything seems fine the next year. There are no disasters to report. If you stop to think about it, the reason is obvious. Because there are fewer elk, there is plenty of food to go around. But year by year the herd builds up. Before long, the breaking point will again be reached.

# Food and feeding

Various grasses form the main part of an elk's diet. Elk are always on the lookout for the best grasslands.

Because the best grass is usually found in large open areas, the elk became a herd animal. Hundreds of years ago, the animals found that they were safer in herds. There were more eyes to watch for danger from predators. Even though almost all of the elk's natural predators have disappeared, elk still have the herding habit today.

You might think that a large herd would be led by the biggest bull. It isn't. An older female usually is the leader. This is also true of most other herding animals. The cow decides when and what the herd will eat. Bluegrass, bromegrass, and wheatgrass will be high on the list. The bark and twigs of aspen, willows, and various pine trees are eaten as browse. If various wild berries are in season, elk will stop to munch on them, too.

Like domestic cattle, elk are ruminants. Ruminants are animals that fill their stomachs without really chewing the food. This allows them to eat their fill in a hurry. Then they can leave dangerous, open spaces and move into the cover of nearby trees. After lying down to rest, they spit up their food in chunks known as cuds. After chewing each cud, it is swallowed again.

Elk will usually feed at sunrise and again at sunset. In between times they rest. If elk are bothered by people, they will often change their eating habits. They have been known to eat all night and rest during the day.

*Grasses are the main part of an elk's diet.*

*A cow elk stops feeding to take a drink of water in a mountain meadow.*

# The senses

The senses of smell, hearing, and sight (in that order) are the most important senses to an elk. The sense of

*A yearling "spike" bull sniffs the air to sense danger.*

smell is the first line of defense. Just ask anyone that has ever tried to hunt elk. If a person approaches elk with the wind at their back, it would be a miracle if he or she were to catch even a glimpse of a fleeing herd. If there is even a little breeze, a predator's only chance is to approach the herd into the wind.

If there is no wind, the elk use their sense of hearing. It takes the skill of a cat to walk up on an elk on a quiet day. Any unnatural sound, like the snap of a twig, and the elk will be off for parts unknown.

If the elk does have a weakness, it's their eyesight. They are very good at spotting movement of any kind, but they don't seem to notice an object that doesn't move. One of the few tactics that a hunter can use successfully makes use of this fact. The hunter has to quietly ease into an area before sunrise or sunset and sit down. He or she can't move a muscle, except their eyes. The hunter also has to pick an area to watch where the wind would be in their face. Then, if the elk walks by, they could not hear, smell, or see the hunter.

# Elk "talk"

In the introduction we talked about the spine-tingling sound of a bugling bull. The bull uses the bugle sound just like he uses his antlers—to threaten other bulls during the mating season. Usually the bull with the largest antlers also has the most "frightening" bugle.

*A bull elk bugles at dawn during the mating season.*

If the herd bull hears a challenging bugle nearby, he'll often charge off towards the intruder. His intention is to get close enough to the intruder to show off his massive antlers. This usually drives the intruder away from the cows that the herd bull is "protecting."

Except during the fall breeding season, bull elk seldom make a sound. By comparison, the cows do a lot of "talking." They make several sounds. During the breeding season they bugle a bit to keep in touch with the bulls. But their bugle is much, much quieter than the bulls. A cow might squeal if she's angry or can't find her calf. To warn the herd of danger, the lead cow often makes a noise that sounds like a cough or bark.

Elk calves are pretty quiet. They keep in touch with their mothers by making a bleating sound.

Elk also use scent glands to communicate during the breeding season. They have glands around their sex organs and on the insides of their hind legs. These glands give off odors that let other elk know that they are ready to mate.

*Elk have scent glands on their hind legs.*

# CHAPTER THREE:

# Spring: getting together

At the beginning of spring the elk are spread out in the low country. Each cow goes off by herself to feed on the new green shoots of grass. In late May the time to give birth arrives. The cow seeks out dense cover for protection. Cows usually give birth to only one calf. Sometimes, they may have twins.

An elk calf will weigh about twenty-five pounds (11.3 kg) at birth. Even before the cow finishes licking off the protective sac, the calf gets on its feet. The calf's

*A cow licks her calf, as it stands for the first time.*

*A cow watches for danger while her calf nurses.*

rust-colored coat is covered with white spots. The markings will help the calf hide from danger. The cow leads the calf to a safe place whenever she leaves to feed. The calf knows by instinct to lie down, and stay put, until the cow returns. Because the calf does not give off any scent, it is usually safe from predators if it doesn't move.

About a week after birth, the cow and her calf join the other cows that have calves. By this time the calf can run quite well. Sometimes, older cows will "babysit" while the mothers feed. After about one month of nursing, the calves start feeding on grasses with their mothers. Most calves will continue to nurse, off and on, for another two or three months.

Slowly, small herds of cows, calves, and young bulls start working their way up to higher elevations. The older bulls move up by themselves. The spring migration up into the mountains is in much smaller groups than the fall migration down the mountain will be.

# Summer: getting fat

The elk will travel to the highest mountain meadows to find new, tender grasses that are rich in food value. Breezes give relief from the biting insects that are found in the low country. The air currents that rise up the mountain warn the elk of any danger from below. On hot days elk often roll in a cool mountain stream to cool their bodies.

The bulls, especially, will spend a large part of their time eating. Now is the time for them to fatten up. During the coming breeding season, they'll be too busy to eat.

# Fall: the bugling season

The first snow of early fall will cause the elk to move down the mountain a ways to a sheltered valley. Bulls soon begin to feel the mating urge.

The first frosty morning of fall finds the hills echoing with the sounds of bugling. The herd bulls round up

*A bull elk herds his "harem" of cows across a river.*

cows into groups called "harems." The younger bulls spend most of their time running from harem to harem. They're hoping to get into a harem and take away a cow, but they're seldom successful. This wild period lasts for a month or more. The bulls will have lost a lot of weight. When the breeding season is over, they will have to spend much of their time eating to fatten themselves for the coming winter.

# Winter: moving down

As soon as the snow starts to cover the mountain meadows, the elk gather in large herds and move down the mountain. If there's a break in the weather, they'll stop the migration. They don't want to leave the relative safety of the mountain if they don't have to. For this is the hunting season. The elk seem to know that not many people will bother to get far from the roads in the low country. The elk feel safer on the mountain.

Finally, the heavy snows of winter come. The elk have no choice. They have to move down the mountain, or they'll starve. In the past, elk herds often traveled a hundred miles to get to their wintering grounds. But today, most of them just drop down to the bottom of the mountain range that they've been on all summer. Their former migration routes have been shut off by civilization. The elk have to "make do" with what's left for them.

Once on the wintering grounds, most of the elk's time is spent eating. If it's an easy winter and there is plenty of food, the elk will survive. If there's a food shortage or deep snow covering the food, many in the herd might die.

The oldest bulls and the youngest calves will be the first to die in a hard winter. That might seem cruel, but it's nature's way of protecting the herd. It allows the strongest members of the herd to survive.

And after all, the hope of spring, with its rich grasses, is just around the corner.

*The oldest and youngest members of an elk herd will die first when there is a hard winter.*

# CHAPTER FOUR:

# The outlook can be good

By the early 1900's an original herd of ten million North American elk had shrunk to less than 100,000 animals. Today there are almost 500,000 elk in North America. If not a miracle, the rebuilding of the elk herd is perhaps as close as one can get.

But there is a problem with all this success. Some areas have too many elk. The range just cannot support them. People have to learn that you can't keep having more elk, if you don't have more areas in which to put them.

If anything, this problem will continue to get worse. More and more people want to make use of the mountains. Mining companies want to move into areas that have been previously closed to them. Development companies are building houses and resorts in the mountains. All of these activities just squeeze the elk into smaller areas. Smaller ranges lead to fewer elk.

In short, we've got to decide whether we want creature comforts or elk. If we don't start listening to the warnings of game-management experts pretty soon, elk may once again decrease in numbers. If we act wisely, and save habitat for them, the elk will be just fine. The choice is ours to make.

*If we act wisely, the outlook for the elk can be good.*

# MAP:

▨ **Present distribution of elk
in North America**

▨ **Original distribution of elk**

# INDEX/GLOSSARY:

**BROWSE** 28 — *Shrubs and trees eaten by members of the deer family.*

**BULL** 14, 17, 20 — *A mature male elk.*

**CALF** 17 — *An elk in its first year.*

**CARTILAGE** 22 — *A firm material that is not as hard as bone. Human ears and noses are made of cartilage.*

**CHARACTERISTICS** 32 — *The things that make a person, place or animal special.*

**COW** 17 — *A mature female elk.*

**CROWN** 22 — *A group of small points at the end of a bull Roosevelt elk's antlers.*

**CUD** 28 — *A chunk of partly digested food.*

**DECIDUOUS** 12 — *Trees that have leaves.*

**DEWCLAWS** 18 — *The two outside "toes" on the back of an elk's foot.*

**EXTINCT** 12, 13 — *An animal that no longer exists.*

**FORAGE** 23 — *The food that an elk eats; also the act of eating.*

**HABITAT** 15 — *The place where an animal lives.*

**HAREM** 41 — *A group of cows controlled by a bull during the mating season.*

**MOLT** 18 — *To change from a winter coat to a summer coat of fur.*

**POINTS** 17 — *The branches of a bull elk's antlers.*

**PREDATOR** 27, 28 — *An animal that eats other animals.*

**RANGE** 12, 13 — *The area in which an animal can naturally survive.*

**RUMINANT** 28 — *Animals that chew a cud.*

**ROYAL** 22 — *A bull elk with special crown-shaped points on the ends of its antlers.*

**SAC** 37 — *The covering in which a calf is born.*

**SPIKES** 21 — *A bull elk's first set of antlers, which are a pair of single beams.*

**TRAIL HEAD** 6 — *The beginning of a trail into the mountains.*

**TRANSPLANT** 15 — *To move from one area to another.*

**VELVET** 22 — *The soft covering that protects an antler while it is growing.*

**VESTIGIAL** 18 — *Things that are no longer useful.*

**WILDERNESS** 12 — *Large areas of land where no people live.*

**YEARLING** 21 — *An elk in its second year.*

47

**WILDLIFE**
*HABITS & HABITAT*

**READ AND ENJOY THE SERIES:**

If you would like to know more about all kinds of wildlife, you should take a look at the other books in this series.

You'll find books on bald eagles and other birds. Books on alligators and other reptiles. There are books about deer and other big-game animals. And there are books about sharks and other creatures that live in the ocean.

In all of the books you will learn that life in the wild is not easy. But you will also learn what people can do to help wildlife survive. So read on!